# A Taste of Serendib

A Sri Lankan Cookbook

by Mary Anne Mohanraj

illustrated by Rachel Hartman

A Taste of Serendib. © 2003 by Mary Anne Mohanraj. All rights reserved. Printed in the United States of America. No part of this book may be used or reproduced in any manner whatsoever without written permission except in the case of brief quotations embedded in critical articles or reviews.

Lethe Press
102 Heritage Avenue
Maple Shade, NJ  08052
www.lethepress.com

Cover illustration by Rachel Hartman (www.amyunbounded.com)
Cover design by Zak Jarvis (www.voidmonster.com)

Text set in Times New Roman and Papyrus. Ornaments set in Hoefler Text Ornaments.

For my mother, who can
somehow use the exact
same recipe I do, yet
make it taste ten times
better, for my father, who
makes quite decent
scrambled eggs,
and for my sisters, fine
cooks themselves,
getting finer every day.

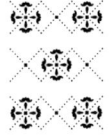

# Acknowledgements

Jae Leslie Adams, Todd Belton, Edward Burke, Shannon John Clark, Beth Jane Freeman, Lou Hoffman, David Horwich, Naomi Kritzer, Alexis Glynn Latner, Deborah A. Levinson, Joanna Lowenstein, Parvati Madduri, Elaine Martyn, Mirna Mohanraj, Sharmila Mohanraj, Kimberly Richards, Karen Schaffer, Nathan Soza, Karen Swanberg, Kelly Williams – my fabulous test cooks. These dishes wouldn't even have been readable without their skillful assistance.

# Contents

### Introduction
Sri Lankan Cooking, from America ...... 11
A Few Caveats ................................ 20
Sri Lankan Meals ............................ 21
Notes for Vegetarians ...................... 23
Photos and Additional Comments ...... 23
Spices and Ingredients ..................... 23
Sri Lankan Curry Powder ................. 27

### Appetizers and Snacks
*Fish (or Ground Beef, or Vegetable) Cutlets* ....... *31*
*Tangy Shrimp on Toast* ..................... *33*
*Curried Mushroom Spread* ................. *34*
*Chicken and Meat Patties* .................. *35*
*Curry Buns (Meat or Vegetable)* ......... *38*

### Meat and Poultry
*Spicy Beef and Potatoes* ..................... *41*
*Spicy Chicken Curry* ......................... *42*
*Ginger-Garlic Chicken* ...................... *44*
*Chili Eggs* ....................................... *45*

### Fish and Seafood
*Crab Curry* ...................................... *49*
*Tamarind Shrimp Curry* ..................... *51*
*Mackerel Curry* ................................ *52*

### Vegetables
*Curried Beets* ................................... *58*
*Carrots and Green Bean Curry* ............ *59*
*Cauliflower Curry* ............................. *60*
*Mixed Vegetable Curry* ...................... *61*
*Potatoes, Peas, and Tomatoes* ............ *62*
*Spicy Potato Curry* ........................... *63*
*Lemon-Masala Mushrooms* ................ *64*
*Chana Masala (Chickpeas)* ................. *65*
*Red Lentils with Spices* ..................... *66*

# Contents (cont.)

**Accompaniments**
- Scallion Scrambled Eggs ................................. 72
- Coconut Sambol................................................ 73
- Seeni (Sugar) Sambol........................................ 74
- Fried Eggplant Sambol ..................................... 75
- Cabbage Mallung................................................ 76
- Leeks Fried with Chili ...................................... 77
- Rasam.................................................................. 78
- Kiri Hodhi (Coconut Milk Gravy)...................... 79
- Cucumber-Tomato Raita..................................... 80
- Mango-Ginger Chutney ..................................... 81

**Rice and Breads**
- Golden Rice Pilaf............................................... 85
- Vegetable or Chicken Biryani ........................... 86
- Pittu .................................................................... 87
- Uppuma ............................................................... 88
- Kottu Roti........................................................... 89
- Hoppers............................................................... 90
- Stringhoppers..................................................... 92

**Drinks**
- Mango Lassi ....................................................... 97
- Falooda................................................................ 98
- Chai Tea ............................................................ 100

**Sweets**
- Milk Toffee........................................................ 103
- Vattalappam (Spiced Coconut Custard)........... 104
- Lemon-Chai Rice Pudding ............................... 105
- Rich Cake .......................................................... 106
  (Wedding/Christmas Cake)

# Introduction

Sri Lankan Cooking, from America
A Few Caveats
Sri Lankan Meals
Notes for Vegetarians
Photos and Additional Comments
Spices and Ingredients

### Sri Lankan Cooking, from America

Make sure you have enough onions. This is critical. You always need more onions than you think you do. A three-pound bag might be enough — better to get two, just to be safe. When I first started cooking, in college, my roommates were amazed by how many onions I bought. They would flee the kitchen while I was chopping, their eyes burning. And when it came time to cook the chili powder ("fry it 'til it makes you cough"), they flung open windows, or left the apartment altogether. But they always came back to eat when the meal was ready.

College wasn't really the first time I cooked. It was just the first time I cooked entire meals — and also the first time I cooked for anyone outside my family. I was at the University of Chicago, many states away from Connecticut, and it wasn't long before bland dorm food (not as bad as everyone claimed, but so boring!) had driven me to trying to reproduce my mother's curries. It wasn't easy — she had never formally taught me how to cook.

What she did have me do, growing up, was chop onions. That's the first kitchen task I remember; I must have been about twelve or so when she first trusted me with a sharp knife. She set me up at the cutting board with the knife and three onions, enough for a single dish. She showed me how to cut off the ends, slice the onion in half, peel it. Then she had me slicing the length of the onion, as thinly as I could. When an onion half is sliced, you turn it, holding it firmly, and cut crosswise, making a fine dice. Practice until you can do this quickly — despite what you may hear about keeping onions cold in the fridge, or about putting a slice of bread on your head to suck up the fumes, cutting them quickly is the only way I know to effectively reduce the tears, every time.

I never cut them as finely as she did; I wasn't a particularly conscientious teenager, and often my chopping was more a matter of five cuts along the onion's length, rather than ten, or fifteen, or more. Mostly my mother put up with my coarsely-chopped onions, though occasionally she'd take the board away and finish the job herself, her knife flying across the board, neat mounds of tiny onion pieces piling up. When finished chopping, she would slide the onions into a large pot, add two large cooking spoons of vegetable oil, and start sautéing them on high. Once I grew halfway competent at chopping onions, she started me stirring them.

Chopping and stirring — these seemed the most tedious parts of cooking, and they were all I was allowed to do. My mother was careful when she cooked — she wasn't satisfied when a few pieces were sliced too large, or when there was the least hint of brown on the onions (which should only sauté until they're a translucent pale gold). I bored easily back then, so I usually stirred the onions with a book in my hand, to relieve the tedium. Sometimes, that meant that they burned a little. As a teenager, I couldn't understand what the fuss was about — it tasted good enough, didn't it, even if the onions turned somewhat brown? What was the problem?

We came to America when I was about two and a half. I grew up in Connecticut, eating cereal or toast for breakfast, a cold cut sandwich or a mass-produced hot meal at school for lunch. My parents were careful with money — we had fast food only after church on

Sunday (and argued over whether we were going to McDonald's or KFC), and only ate out at real restaurants on a birthday or other special occasion. So mostly, I had very simple American food during the day, and I had rice and curry every night — usually plain white rice, a meat curry, and a vegetable. If we had guests then we might have appetizers (fish cutlets, meat rolls), more vegetables, more meat, accompaniments (chutneys, sambols). But most days — rice, chicken or beef, green beans or cauliflower or carrots. These days, I tend to eat a different ethnic cuisine every night, but growing up, I was never bored with my mother's menu. It was always a little different, and it was always so good.

A lot of people think their mom is the best cook in the world. I won't claim that, but I do know that my mother was and is considered a *very* good cook, not just by me, but by everyone we knew. Part of it was that she had the time for it, of course — my father worked, and she raised us. She kept a spotless house, and took similar care with her cooking. Some of my friends' mothers also cooked with the same sort of care. But as I grew up, I knew fewer and fewer people who cooked like that — fewer people who really cared how finely the onions were diced, how long they'd been sautéing. Most of my college friends couldn't cook at all — or if they could, they could only do spaghetti. If they were brave enough to sauté a little ground beef to toss into the store-bought sauce, they were culinary wonders. They really knew how to cook!

So in college, I started trying to cook too. I called up my mother, and asked her for her beef and potato recipe (still my favorite). I admit to resenting the fact that I had to ask; I was frustrated that she hadn't somehow, magically, infused her cooking ability into me. But eventually I realized that it would have been difficult for her to teach me to cook; I spent most of my teenage time either studying, reading novels, or talking on the phone with friends. I had plans for my future, plans that were focused on a good college, a serious career. I wasn't going to be a housewife! If she had tried to get me to sit still long enough to teach me a dish from start to finish, I would have undoubtedly complained. I know I complained about all that onion chopping and frying.

I couldn't make the dish properly at first — I didn't have the right spices for meat. It wasn't just a matter of going to the grocery store and buying chili powder — and I definitely didn't want to buy what they called curry powder! The yellow curry powder you find at the store is fine for North Indian cooking, but it's nothing like what we use. In Sri Lanka, the spices are dry roasted separately and then ground and mixed together. They become dark and very aromatic; it's a flavor completely unlike what you'd get from using Indian curry powder, and the dishes turn out a dark brown, rather than a pale yellow. These days, I take the time to go to the Indian grocery store, buy bulk spices, and make my own Sri Lankan curry powder — it's easy with a coffee grinder dedicated to spice grinding, and a pleasant way to spend a mellow half-hour, slowly roasting the spices, stirring them occasionally. Back then, I waited for my dad to pack up some curry powder and send it along. (*Sri Lankan Curry Powder, page 23*)

I started simple at first — I just made beef and potato curry, my favorite. I made that for two whole years — I didn't cook anything else. My friends often don't believe that I use ketchup in that recipe; it doesn't seem authentic to them. But my mother often cooked with ketchup, which is really just a blend of tomatoes, vinegar and sugar. It sped up the process, and I figure if it's good enough for her, it's good enough for me. You can substitute tomatoes and vinegar for the ketchup in that beef recipe up above if it makes you feel better; it won't blend as well, though.

My junior year, I had one roommate who loved curry (the other couldn't take spicy food at all), and I had met this guy, Kevin, who was sort of seeing someone else, but who would come and hang out sometimes; he could eat hotter food that I could. I would make a big pot of this curry, and we would sit on the floor with a loaf of sliced white bread (it makes the best curry sandwiches, honestly), eating right out of the pot, talking until all hours of the night, flirting. My mother would have seriously disapproved of the flirting. But with practice, the curry got to be pretty good; she would have been pleased with that, at least. *(Beef and Potato Curry, page 37)*

I might have continued on like that — just a single beef curry to my name. I knew a few other dishes along with the beef curry, standard college student staples: spaghetti, ramen, scrambled eggs, and rice. That summed up my culinary expertise. And even the rice could be difficult — I managed to forget it on the stove one time, went off to class, and came back a few hours later to find that it had charred into a lava-like mass, and had set off the fire alarm for the entire twelve-story dorm. But I mastered rice in time, and I was pretty proud of my cooking skills for a while; I cooked more than most of my friends. Then I became good friends with Karina — a vegetarian. She wasn't about to even try my beef curry! And not long after we met, Kevin (whom I was now seriously dating) went vegetarian too (although it didn't stick with him).

I was still in college but now a junior, in a shared suite with a kitchen; I cooked many of my meals. I had been living mostly on that beef curry, but it wasn't going to work for them. So I called my mom again. I was pretty sure I remembered eating vegetables when I was a kid, at least some of the time. I was dubious about being able to make entire meals out of them, but I was willing to try... *(Green Bean and Carrot Curry, page 51)*

It turned out that there was basically one recipe that you could use for carrots, or beets, or bell peppers — a yellow vegetable curry, good for almost any vegetable you want to throw in there. That kept us going for a while. But eventually Karina started to wistfully ask for a little variety...maybe some protein? Back to my mother, who produced chili eggs. *(Chili Eggs, page 40)* I now knew enough dishes to actually put together an entire meal, or even throw a small dinner party; I was starting to feel like I could really cook!

So now I could cook meat dishes (chicken can be cooked much the same as beef, and for fish, you just add a teaspoon of tamarind paste) and vegetable dishes. But even though I loved Sri Lankan food, I didn't want to eat it every night — I started experimenting with other cuisines, buying cookbooks, eventually looking for recipes on-line. As I got older, I started wanting to have people over for dinner; I wanted nice plates on the table, linen napkins, flowers.

I'm not sure where the urge to entertain came from, though I wouldn't be surprised if some of it was based on the memory of the huge dinner parties my mom would have when I was growing up, where she would start cooking a week ahead of time, making the curries and refrigerating them (they only get better with time), so they could all be reheated just before the meal. I didn't get quite that extravagant, but I did finally make enough money that I could afford to have people come for dinner every other week or so — and when they did, I wanted to make them meals that they would remember, that they would talk about for days, the way people talked about my mother's chicken curry, her fish cutlets, her coconut sambols, her biryani rice.

I still don't cook as well as my mother did, not reliably. For years, I tended to take too many shortcuts — I'd come home tired from work, and I didn't care whether I had chopped the onions finely enough; I just wanted to eat! But over time, I grew more and more dissatisfied with some of those shortcuts; if I was going to take the time to cook, I wanted to do it right. If I couldn't be bothered to make the effort, then I should just order pizza and be done with it. That attitude must have come from my mother, who spent hours cutting carrots into tiny slivers. We had a food processor, but hardly ever used it. Skilled hands did a better job.

I admit to using a few shortcuts, though — for example, real biryani rice takes a lot of time and effort. My mother would chop many ingredients finely (onions, carrots, etc.) and fry them each separately (sometimes chopping for so long that her hands developed knife blisters). She would make a mild chicken curry and cook it down. She'd stir it all together into the cooked rice, and then bake the whole thing so the flavors melded. Her chicken biryani took forever to make, and I just wasn't willing to spend the time. But I realized I could use some of the elements to make a twenty minute rice pilaf that would taste good and impress my friends. And while the rice was cooking, I could set the table, and make a coconut sambol to accompany the meal. (*Rice Pilaf, page 77; Coconut Sambol, page 65)*

I work as a writer now. I write fiction, poetry, essays. I've been writing for about twelve years — about as long as I've been cooking. And as I get older, I find that I care about quality. I'm willing to work at my writing, at my cooking, willing to study it in order to get the best possible results. I enjoy learning about food; what once seemed like work now seems like pleasure, and I make the time to cook carefully because I know that I (and my friends) will appreciate the results. I'm more patient in my thirties than I was in my twenties, more willing to stir on low heat if that's what the dish requires, rather than turning it up to a quick high. I chop my onions as finely as required. I hardly ever read while I'm stirring. I've learned that sometimes multi-tasking does more harm than good.

But at the same time, I don't really cook as painstakingly as my mother does. I look for ways I can shorten cooking times and ease dull tasks, without sacrificing too much flavor. Sometimes I compromise a little on flavor if it makes the overall process more pleasurable. Serving good food is a pleasure, but if I don't also enjoy the preparation of it, then it comes at too high a price for me. I won't cut carrots until my fingers blister; that probably means that I'll never be as good a cook as my mother is. That's okay.

There's probably quite a lot in my life that I don't do the way my mother would recommend — but there are some skills that I received directly from her. I can go through a three-pound bag of onions without blinking — okay, maybe I blink quite a bit, but the fumes don't send me running from the kitchen. My fingers have long ago learned their lessons, and after all those hours of chopping, I can now dice onions as finely as my mother can (though still not quite as fast). When I have the time, and am willing to spend it, I do know how to cook, which strikes me as a great gift, and one that I can never repay her for.

I can only begin to repay that gift by passing on as much as I know. There's far more to Sri Lankan cooking than is contained in these pages — but this is as much as I currently know. I hope you enjoy these dishes, that they pique your interest, that you go on to learn more, that you experiment with them, that you have fun. And when the onion fumes are making the tears run down your face, I hope that you will find the end result worthwhile. I do.

*Start with the onions. Chop them finely, sauté them carefully, start a beef and potato curry. While that simmers, you can make a vegetable dish and the chili eggs, if you work quickly and efficiently. Set the eggs to boiling. Start the vegetable dish, and while the vegetables simmer, make the chili onions for the eggs. Cover them when they're done, and put the rice on, about twenty minutes before you want to eat. Stir everything periodically — don't let it burn. Paying attention is important. Make a coconut sambol, and while the flavors in it are melding, set the table. Light some candles. Transfer your curries into serving dishes and set them on the table. Load the dirty pots into the dishwasher and close the door — you can deal with it later. No one will know. Pour yourself a glass of wine, and open the door to your guests. And when you're done eating, there's no need for a fancy dessert*

*— some fresh fruit over ice cream will be perfect. In two hours, with practice, you can cook a terrific meal for six. And you can enjoy doing it, which is at least as important as whether you made it perfectly.*

## A Few Caveats

I learned to cook from watching my mother; I would ask her how to make a dish, and she would say, "Just watch." So I did, and I wrote things down, and sometimes I would pester her with questions — when she tossed in some black mustard seed, I'd ask her how much she'd put in, and when she answered "three pinches", I'd try to estimate what that meant in teaspoons. I've tried to convert to standard measurements when I can, for your convenience (and if you need metric, I recommend using Google's built-in metric converter — if you tell it 3 cups, it'll tell you how many grams).

But I wouldn't recommend being too tied to the precise measurements in the recipes; learning from my mother, I quickly found that it wasn't much use, trying to write down exact recipes. When I started cooking, I found that the appropriate amounts often varied from day to day, depending on a strange chemistry of interactions that I am not skilled enough to describe. Don't be afraid to add a little less chili powder, or a little more milk or ketchup, or vice versa!

I also started experimenting, and so I must warn you that many of the recipes in this book are not strictly Sri Lankan — they are simply what I cook, when I'm cooking the food that makes me happiest. If you're looking for authentic dishes, I would strongly recommend Charmaine Solomon's Sri Lankan section in her *Complete Asian Cookbook*, which I turn to often, or you might try *The Food of Sri Lanka* (Douglas Bullis and Wendy Hutton), which contains recipes collected from the island's finest restaurants.

Finally, please keep in mind that the food I grew up with is that of the Tamil minority in Sri Lanka, which is primarily Hindu. My own family has been largely Catholic, as a legacy of the Portuguese influence. We had no cultural/religious strictures against eating meat, and were, of course, encouraged to eat quite a lot of fish, especially on Friday. Our cuisine is similar to that of the Tamil Nadu province in India, though, of course, with some specifically Sri Lankan differences. The majority of the island is populated by Sinhalese, who are largely Buddhist, and often vegetarian — their cuisine is quite different from what you'll find in these pages.

## Sri Lankan Meals

We came to America when I was two years old, and so I never ate like a Sri Lankan would in Sri Lanka; for example, I had usually cereal for breakfast growing up in Connecticut. A typical Sri Lankan breakfast is a little rice with some curry, or with lentils. (I dislike lentils and never learned to cook them, so I'm afraid they're rather absent from this book, but most people in Sri Lanka eat lots of them). If you were feeling fancier, you might make hoppers (but you'd have to plan that the night before). Uppuma is also a nice change, usually with some fish curry. (I've actually gotten addicted to eating American pancakes with curry; the sweetness of the pancakes works really well with a spicy curry. The *Fannie Farmer* cookbook has a solid pancake recipe).

Usually I would have a bologna sandwich for lunch, but in Sri Lanka, lunches are rice and curries, usually eaten around 3 p.m., and dinners are the same, usually eaten around 9 p.m. Generally we would serve plain white rice, a meat curry, and a vegetable curry. Appetizers and sides are usually saved for when guests or more family come over, although you might keep a container of sambol around, just for a little added flavor. Some of my American friends are surprised when I tell them that I had rice and curry for dinner every single night when I was growing up — what can I say? If your mother is an excellent cook, then you never get bored with it.

The fancier dishes, the hoppers and pittu and stringhoppers, the patties and cutlets, the milk toffees and rich cake — those were all saved for parties. Usually, we stuffed ourselves on the delectable appetizers, but somehow always managed to find a little room for dinner and then dessert.

Do keep in mind that in Sri Lanka, we'd always eat rice and curry with our nice clean hands (actually, just the right hand). I swear, it's tastier that way – and if you're cooking meat on the bone, it's a lot easier than trying to manage utensils. If you're having a dinner party, you can always provide small rinsing bowls at the side of each plate for people to wash off their fingers.

And finally, be aware that most Sri Lankans don't generally drink wine with their meals; if you do want to serve wine, I'd recommend a dry Gewürztraminer or Riesling, or a sturdy Merlot.

## Notes for Vegetarians

Sri Lankan Tamil cooking is oriented around meat and fish; vegetable dishes are primarily meant to accompany a central meat dish. But many of the meat dishes here do work fine with meat substitutes, such as seitan, tofu, and meat-simulators (such as the "Ground Meatless" from Morningstar Farms or the "Diced Chik" from Worthington). Also, if you freeze tofu, then thaw it and break it into pieces, it gives it a chewy texture; you can also deep-fry it, which is delicious but does make it soak up quite a lot of fat. An alternative to deep frying is to cut the tofu into rectangles or squares, lay them in an oiled pan in a single layer, then spray them lightly with spray oil and bake until golden brown. And of course, adding lentils or chickpeas to any vegetable dish is a good way to get added protein. They should work particularly well in the potato curry, for example.

## Photos and Additional Comments

We're pleased to note that we'll be including a web component to this book, with photos of many of the recipes and an online forum where cooks can ask each other questions and exchange tips. You can find it at: http://www.mamohanraj.com/Taste/taste.html.

## Spices and Ingredients

**Agar-agar** is a seaweed powder, which works much like plain gelatin. You can often find it at a large organic gourmet store, like Whole Foods, or possibly at your local Indian grocery store.

If you can't find **black (or brown) mustard seed**, regular mustard seed will do.

Buy your **chili powder** at the Indian grocery store — it should be a dark red. If you can't get to such a store, use cayenne — Mexican chili powder (a mix of several spices) is not a good substitute.

Watch for this symbol – it'll tell you which dishes are spicy. To adjust spiciness, increase or decrease the amount of chili powder or chili peppers.

**Curry leaves** are broad, flat, dark-green leaves, thumb-sized or larger, which can be found in a good Indian grocery store, either fresh or dried. If you buy fresh, they'll keep frozen for quite a long time. There is no good substitute — if you can't find them, leave them out of the recipe. The thin, rounded silvery leaves of the curry plant you can occasionally find at garden stores are not meant for cooking — they merely smell curry-like.

Sri Lankan cooking is generally hotter than Indian, so if you're not used to it, trying making the recipe with only half the roasted **curry powder** (page 27) and/or chili powder the first time around.

Never buy your **desiccated coconut** in the baking aisle — it's almost certainly sweetened. Try the Indian grocery store or organic market instead.

**Fenugreek** is the same as methi seed, which you can generally find in an Indian grocery store (where, incidentally, most spices will be much cheaper than in your general grocery store).

**Ghee** is clarified butter (pure butter fat without any of the milk solids), and can be bought in Indian grocery stores. It can be heated to much higher temperatures than butter without burning, and has a distinctive flavor.

When a recipe calls for **green chilies**, it's asking for Thai green chilies, which are slender and about a finger-length long. They're quite hot, so if you can't find them and substitute in something like jalapeño, you'll want to use more chili in the rest of the dish.

Many of the recipes call for a little **milk** — my mother generally used whole milk, or coconut milk if she was cooking for a party; coconut milk is a little sweeter and much richer in taste due to the high fat content. You can sometimes find light coconut milk, which is still very tasty. I usually use 2% or 1% or even skim milk myself; they'll all work fine — I've also used rice milk and soy milk when cooking for vegans, and while the sauce won't thicken quite as much, it still basically works.

**Panch Phoron** is a five-spice mix, consisting of equal parts of cumin seed, black mustard seed, fennel seed, fenugreek/methi seed, and black cumin seed – it can be bought at Indian groceries, or mixed yourself at home.

You can buy **rose water** in Indian grocery stores — and if you can't find that, you can dilute **rose essence** in water to make it. Just be careful — the essence is extremely strong. A few drops should suffice for a cup of water. And similarly, a cup of pre-made rose water should be roughly equal to 2-3 drops of rose essence in a cup of water.

**Tamarind**, a tangy fruit, comes in many forms — blocks of hard paste, fresh pods, dried pods — and the form I prefer, a soft paste which comes in a small jar (generally with a red lid). Again, the Indian grocery store is your friend.

**Tulsi seeds** are tiny black seeds which develop a slippery, translucent coat when soaked in water; they are flavorless, but some people like the texture. Others can't stand them, and think they're slimy.

And if you live in the middle of nowhere, you really need to know about Penzey's (www.penzeys.com) Spices — varied, fresh, delicious. Their **Tellicherry black pepper** is particularly pungent and potent.

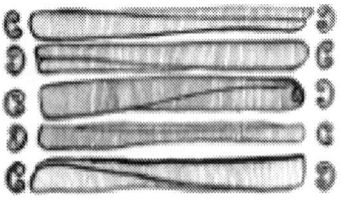

## Sri Lankan Curry Powder

One of the main characteristics of Sri Lankan cooking is that the spices are dark roasted. This gives them an aroma and flavor that is completely different from Indian curries, and you cannot simply substitute yellow curry powder!

- 1 c. coriander seeds
- 1/2 c. cumin seeds
- 1 T fennel seeds
- 1 rounded t. fenugreek (methi) seeds
- 1 cinnamon stick, about 2 inches
- 1 rounded t. whole cloves
- 1 rounded t. cardamom seeds
- 2 T dried curry leaves
- 2 rounded t. red chili powder

1. In a dry pan over medium heat, roast separately the coriander, cumin, fennel and fenugreek, stirring constantly until each one becomes a fairly dark brown. Do not attempt to save time by roasting them together — they each have different cooking times and you will only end up half-cooking some and burning others.

2. Put into blender container (I use a coffee grinder that is dedicated solely to spice grinding) together with cinnamon stick broken in pieces, the cloves, cardamom and curry leaves.

3. Blend at high speed until finely powdered. Sieve into a bowl, discarding any large pieces, and combine with chili powder; stir well. Store in airtight jar.

# Appetizers

Fish (or Ground Beef, or Vegetable) Cutlets
Curried Mushroom Spread
Tangy Shrimp on Toast
Chicken and Meat Patties

## Fish (or Ground Beef, or Vegetable) Cutlets
(90 min. — serves dozens)

Some Americans find these too fishy, but I love them. Over the years, my family has come up with adaptations to suit the tastes of those (like Kevin) who dislike fish, and they've even come up with a variation for vegetarians. But honestly, the mackerel ones are the tastiest.

1 15 oz. can mackerel
1 large russet potato
2 medium yellow onions, chopped fine
1/2 t. black mustard seed
1/2 t. cumin seed
1/2 rounded t. salt
1/3 c. lime juice
1 small yellow onion, minced
2 rounded t. finely chopped fresh green chilies
1/2 rounded t. ground black pepper
1 egg, beaten
dry breadcrumbs, for coating
oil for deep frying

1. Drain fish thoroughly, removing as much liquid as possible. While fish are draining, boil the potatoes, peel, and mash them. Clean the fish, removing scales and bones, and break it into small pieces.

2. Sauté onions with cumin and black mustard seed. Add fish, salt, and lime juice, and cook until very dry (this process reduces the fishy smell, and the drier you get the mixture, the less excess oil they'll pick up when frying). Let cool.

## Fish Cutlets (cont.)

3. Using your hands, mix thoroughly the fish, mashed potatoes, raw onion, black pepper, and chilies. Shape the mixture into small balls, about the size of a cupped palm.

4. Roll each ball in beaten egg, and then roll each ball in the dry breadcrumbs. Fry a few at a time in deep hot oil over medium heat — not too hot! This should take a minute or so each. When well-browned, lift out with a slotted spoon and drain on a metal rack placed over a few layers of paper towels.

*For ground beef cutlets:* For 1 lb. lean ground beef, when you sauté the 2 chopped onions, add 1-2 heaping t. red chili powder and 1/2 c. ketchup, as well as the 1/2 rounded t. salt from above. Add the ground beef (skipping the lime juice), and fry until very dry, draining any excess oil. Skip the raw onion, chilies, and black pepper — proceed otherwise as for the fish cutlets.

*For vegetable cutlets:* Use 1 lb. frozen mixed vegetables, thawed (you might have to cut up the green beans into smaller pieces). Sauté the onions, mustard seed, and cumin seed as for the fish; add the vegetables and salt and cook until very dry. Skip the raw onion if you like, but definitely stir in an extra 1/2 t. of salt when you mix the veggies in with the potatoes, black pepper, and chilies. Proceed otherwise as for the fish cutlets.

## Curried Mushroom Spread
(30 min. — serves dozens)

This dish is entirely my own invention; I became frustrated trying to have dinner parties, because so many of our appetizers are deep-fried — delicious, but not so good for you. This didn't actually end up being all that healthy, given the cream. Ah well.

   2 lbs. mushrooms, sliced or chopped
   2 large yellow onions, chopped fine
   several T butter — add as needed
   1-2 rounded t. Sri Lankan curry powder
   1/2 - 1 c. heavy cream
   salt and pepper to taste

1. Sauté onions in butter until golden; add mushrooms and sauté on high heat, reducing as much liquid as possible. Add more butter as necessary. When mushrooms are well-reduced, add curry powder, salt, and pepper; mix well.

2. Add heavy cream, turn down heat to low, and simmer until well-blended and cream is reduced, about 5-10 minutes. Check seasonings, adjust if needed. Remove from heat and let cool.

3. Spoon mixture into food processor and pulse until well blended and of a spreading consistency, suitable for mounding on crackers.

*Note:* Mango chutney mixed with cream cheese is also a tasty cracker spread.

## Tangy Shrimp on Toast
(30 min. — serves dozens)

This one presents beautifully, and is surprisingly quick for such a pretty result. I often have an early guest assemble these while I finish off the other dishes – a fun way to include them in the meal.

> 1 lb. small raw, peeled shrimp
> 2 medium yellow onions, minced
> enough vegetable oil to sauté (about 3 T)
> 1-2 rounded t. (to taste) chili powder
> ketchup to taste (about 1/4 c.)
> 1/2 - 1 rounded t. salt
> curly parsley for garnish

1. Sauté onions in oil until golden; add chili powder and sauté on high a minute or two until darkened.

2. Add shrimp, ketchup, and salt; turn down heat to medium and cook, stirring, until well-blended.

3. Serve on crackers, placing 1-2 pieces of shrimp on each cracker and garnishing with a sprig of parsley on top.

*Note:* For fancier (and more time-consuming) presentation, cut small rounds of white bread in advance and toast; dab toasts with butter (butter mixed with a little mustard is even better) and proceed as in 3 above.

## Chicken and Meat Patties
(2-3 hrs. — serves dozens)

One of the images I think of as most typical of Sri Lankan cooking is that of my mother and aunts sitting up late into the night before a big party, assembling patties or rolls or some other appetizer (which they called 'short eats') and talking a mile a minute. The guys really missed out – they were usually discussing politics in the living room, not nearly as much fun.

*Patty pastry:*
2 c. plain flour
1/2 t. salt
3 T butter
1/4 c. thick coconut milk
2 egg yolks, beaten
peanut oil for frying

*Filling:*
1 lb. chicken
1 lb. beef or lamb
8 oz. pork
4 oz. bacon or ham
1 T ghee or butter
1 medium onion, chopped fine
2 t. Sri Lankan curry powder
1 t. ground turmeric
1/4 t. ground cloves
1/4 t. ground cinnamon
1/2 t. ground black pepper
1 1/2 t. salt
2 strips lemon rind
1/2 c. thick coconut milk
2 rounded t. finely chopped fresh dill

## Chicken and Meat Patties (cont.)

1. Make filling: Put chicken, beef and pork into a saucepan with just enough water to cover, bring to a boil, cover and simmer for 20 minutes. Cool. Remove the parboiled chicken meat from the bones and cut into small dice. Do the same with the beef and pork. Reserve stock.

2. Remove rind from bacon and cut into small squares.

3. Heat ghee or butter in a saucepan and fry onions until onions are soft and start to brown. Add the curry powder, turmeric, cloves, cinnamon, pepper, and salt and stir well. Add about 1 1/2 c. of the leftover stock. Add lemon rind and the diced meat. Mix well, cover and simmer gently until meats are tender and liquid almost evaporated.

4. Add the coconut milk and dill, stir, and cook uncovered until coconut milk is absorbed.

5. Remove from heat. When cool, pick out the lemon rind and the curry leaves.

6. Make pastry: Sift flour and salt into a bowl and rub in the butter with your fingertips. Add the coconut milk and egg yolks mixed together and knead lightly to a smooth dough. If necessary add a little extra milk or flour.

## Chicken and Meat Patties (cont.)

7. Wrap dough in greaseproof paper and chill for 30 minutes.

8. Take one quarter of the dough at a time and roll out very thinly on lightly floured board. Cut into circles using a large cookie cutter about 3 inches in diameter.

9. Put a teaspoonful of the filling and a piece of hard-boiled egg on the pastry rounds. Fold over to make a half circle and press edges firmly together to seal. Ornament the edge by pressing with a key or the tines of a fork.

10. When all the patties are made, deep fry a few at a time in hot oil. (Alternatively, brush with egg wash – one egg beaten with one T water – and bake on a cookie sheet at 400 for 20 min.) Drain on layers of paper towels over a cooling rack; serve warm.

*Note:* These can be made ahead and refrigerated (or frozen) — reheat in a 350 degree oven. Call also be made up through step 9 and then frozen to finish cooking on the day of your party.

## Curry Buns (Meat or Vegetable)
(2-3 hrs. — serves dozens)

These are perfect picnic food, car food, party food — they're fabulous. The street vendors in Sri Lanka sell them for a few rupees (about 10 cents or so), which makes it easy to justify buying lots and lots. You can fill them with other curries too.

  1 quantity beef curry (page 41) or other curry
  2 loaves frozen dough (or make your own — any basic bread dough recipe will do)
  1 egg beaten with 1 T water

1. Cook the curry as you would normally, but then cook it longer, until it's very dry. Allow to cool.

2. Prepare dough according to package. You can use all kinds of frozen dough — dinner roll dough will work, even pastry dough will work (though it'll be extremely buttery). But none of them work as well as frozen loaves. Divide the dough into 30 equal portions.

3. Flatten each portion to a circle, put a spoonful of curry in the center and bring the edges together, pressing to seal.

4. Put buns join downwards on greased baking trays, with a little space between them to allow for rising. Cover with a dry cloth and leave in a warm place for 30-40 minutes or until nearly doubled in bulk.

5. Brush with egg glaze and bake at 400 degrees until golden brown. Can be served hot or cold.

# Meat and Poultry

Spicy Beef and Potatoes
Spicy Chicken Curry
Ginger-Garlic Chicken
Chili Eggs

## Spicy Beef and Potatoes
(1 hr. — serves 6)

When I fly home to Connecticut to my parents' house, nine times out of ten, my mother will be in the kitchen cooking this dish for me, because she knows it's my favorite.

> 5 medium yellow onions, chopped fine
> 3 T vegetable oil
> 1/4 t. black mustard seed
> 1/4 t. cumin seed
> 1-2 rounded t. (to taste) red chili powder
> 1 T Sri Lankan curry powder
> 1.5 lbs. chuck steak, cubed, about 1 in.
> 3 medium baking potatoes, cubed ditto
> 1/3 c. ketchup
> 1 heaping t. salt
> 1/2 c. milk, optional

1. In a large pot, sauté onions in oil on high with mustard seed and cumin seeds until onions are golden/translucent (not brown). Add chili powder and cook 1 minute, until you start to cough. Immediately add curry powder, beef, potatoes, ketchup, and salt.

2. Lower heat to medium and add enough water so the potatoes don't burn. Cover and cook, stirring periodically, until beef and potatoes are cooked through. Add milk if desired to thicken and mellow spice level; stir until well-blended. Serve hot.

*Note:* In Sri Lanka, mutton is often used, and makes a delicious curry; try your local butcher for the meat.

## Spicy Chicken Curry
(1 hr. — serves 8-10)

In the first few years of grad school, hectic with work and living alone, I'd make a big batch of this on Sunday and eat it with rice and vegetables for three days, and then mid-week, I'd make a big batch of fish curry, and eat that for another few days.

- 5 medium yellow onions, chopped fine
- 3 T vegetable oil
- 1/4 t. black mustard seed
- 1/4 t. cumin seed
- 3 whole cloves
- 3 whole cardamom pods
- 1 cinnamon stick, broken into 3 pieces
- 1-2 rounded t. (to taste) red chili powder
- 1 T Sri Lankan curry powder
- 10 pieces chicken, about 2 lbs, skinned and trimmed of fat. (Use legs and thighs — debone them if you must, but they'll be tastier if cooked on the bone. Breast meat isn't nearly as yummy.)
- 1/3 c. ketchup
- 1 heaping t. salt
- 1/2 c. milk, optional
- 1 T lemon juice

1. In a large pot, sauté onions in oil on high with mustard seed, cumin seed, cloves, cardamom pods, and cinnamon pieces, until onions are golden/translucent (not brown). Add chili powder and cook a few minutes, until you start to cough. Immediately add curry powder, chicken, ketchup, and salt.

**Spicy Chicken Curry (cont.)**

2. Lower heat to medium. Cover and cook, stirring periodically, until chicken is cooked through and sauce is thick, about 20-30 minutes. Remove cover, taste, and add milk if desired, to thicken and mellow spice level; stir until well-blended. Add lemon juice; simmer a few additional minutes, stirring. Serve hot.

## Ginger-Garlic Chicken
(90 min. — serves 8-12)

I learned this dish recently; I asked my mother to teach me to make a boneless chicken dish, because Kevin (and my middle sister, and many of my friends) prefer not to have to deal with bones in their food. Me, I think the lovely marrow juices make any extra effort entirely worthwhile — and actually, you can also make it with boned chicken – using 2 lbs. of Cornish game hens, cut up and skinned, is particularly tasty.

> 1 heaping t. Indian ginger powder (somewhat different from standard American ground ginger)
> 1 heaping t. Indian garlic powder (ditto)
> 1 heaping t. turmeric
> 5 shakes salt
> 12 chicken thighs, about 2 lbs., skinned and trimmed of fat, deboned and cut bite-size
> vegetable oil for frying
> 1-2 rounded t. (to taste) red chili powder

1. Mix spices in a large bowl; add chicken pieces and rub with your hands until coated. Marinate 1/2 hr.

2. Heat oil; add chili powder and cook 1 minute.

3. Add chicken and sear on high, turning to brown all sides. Reduce to low and cover; cook approximately 15-20 minutes, until meat is cooked through.

4. Uncover and cook until all the liquid is gone. Tilt pan and push chicken pieces to one side; allow oil to drain to one side for 15 minutes or so. Remove chicken to serving dish and serve warm.

## Chili Eggs
(20 min. — serves 8)

This is one of the easiest dishes in here – and fast! If you're having a dinner party and you start worrying that you don't have enough food (which I admit, I'm slightly paranoid about), you can always whip up a quick batch of chili eggs.

>3 medium yellow onions, sliced
>3 T vegetable oil
>1/4 t. black mustard seed
>1/4 t. cumin seed
>1-2 rounded t. (to taste) red chili powder
>3 T ketchup
>1 rounded t. salt
>8 hard-boiled eggs, peeled and sliced in half

1. Hard-boil eggs. There are many recommended methods for boiling eggs — I start them in cold water, bring it to a boil, turn it down to a simmer, and simmer about 15 minutes.

2. While eggs are boiling, sauté onions in oil on high with mustard seed and cumin seeds until onions are golden/translucent (not brown).

3. Add chili powder and cook 1 minute, until you start to cough. Immediately add ketchup and salt; stir until well-blended and cooked through, about 5 minutes. Remove from heat.

4. Shell cooled, cooked eggs and slice in half. Arrange on a plate and spoon chili onions over, turning gently to coat.

# Fish and Seafood

Crab Curry
Tamarind Shrimp Curry
Mackerel Curry

## Crab Curry
(90 min. — serves 4-6)

I remember, while visiting Sri Lanka, watching the fishermen come back with their morning catch. We'd buy fresh crabs and bring them back to the house; I have a vivid memory from when I was about ten of crabs scuttling about on the kitchen floor, though I can't imagine why they were let out there.

  2 lbs. crab legs (raw or cooked)
  3 medium onions, finely chopped
  6 cloves garlic, finely chopped
  2 rounded t. finely grated ginger
  1/2 rounded t. fenugreek seeds
  10 curry leaves
  3 inch stick cinnamon
  1-2 rounded t. (to taste) red chili powder
  1 rounded t. ground turmeric
  1 1/2 rounded t. salt
  6 c. thin coconut milk (3 c. coconut milk +
     3 c. water)
  3 T lemon juice

1. Remove large shells of crabs and discard fibrous tissue found under the shell. Divide each crab into 4 portions, breaking each body in half and separating large claws from body. Leave legs attached to body.

## Crab Curry (cont.)

2. Put onion, garlic, ginger, fenugreek, curry leaves, cinnamon, chili, turmeric, salt, and thin coconut milk into a large saucepan. Cover and simmer gently 30 minutes. Add crabs and cook for 20 minutes if using raw crabs. Cook for only 5-7 minutes if cooked crabs are used. If pan is not large enough, simmer half the pieces of crab at a time. Crab should be submerged in sauce while cooking.

3. Add lemon juice. Simmer uncovered an additional 10 minutes. Serve hot.

*Note: If you desire a thicker sauce, remove crab to a serving dish, turn up heat, and cook sauce further until it reaches desired thickness; then pour sauce over crab.*

## Tamarind Shrimp Curry

(45 min. — serves 4-6)

My mother makes the curry sauce and then adds shelled, deveined shrimp. But shrimp shells hold a lot of flavor, and this is a classic technique for extracting some of the flavor and saving it for your dish.

   1 lb. raw shrimp, shelled (shells reserved)
   2 c. water
   3 medium yellow onions, chopped fine
   3 T vegetable oil
   1/4 t. black mustard seed
   1/4 t. cumin seed
   1-2 rounded t. (to taste) red chili powder
   1 T Sri Lankan curry powder
   1/3 c. ketchup
   1 heaping t. salt
   1 rounded t. tamarind paste

1. Boil shrimp shells in water 15 minutes or so. Drain, reserving water. Discard shells.

2. Sauté onions in oil on high with mustard seed and cumin seeds until onions are golden/translucent (not brown). Add chili powder and cook 1 minute, until you start to cough. Immediately add curry powder, ketchup, and salt. Stir well.

3. Add reserved shrimp water and bring to a boil. Add tamarind paste and dissolve.

4. Lower heat to medium. Cover and cook, stirring occasionally, until sauce thickens, 20-30 minutes. When sauce is thick and well-reduced, add shrimp and cook until shrimp are firm and pink. Serve hot.

## Mackerel Curry
(40 min. — serves 4-6)

People get scared of this dish because they think mackerel is overly fishy — and food snobs put their noses in the air when they realize we're using canned fish. All I can say in response is that this is one of my all-time favorite dishes.

   3 medium yellow onions, chopped
   3 T vegetable oil
   1/4 t. black mustard seed
   1/4 t. cumin seed
   1-2 rounded t. (to taste) red chili powder
   1 T Sri Lankan curry powder
   1/3 c. ketchup
   1 heaping t. salt
   1 1/2 c. water
   1 rounded t. tamarind paste
   1 14 oz. can mackerel, drained and rinsed
   4 hard-boiled eggs, peeled and sliced in half

1. Sauté onions in oil on high with mustard seed and cumin seeds until onions are golden/translucent (not brown). Add chili powder and cook 1 minute, until you start to cough. Immediately add curry powder, ketchup, and salt. Stir well.

2. Add water and bring to a boil. Add tamarind paste and dissolve. Lower heat to medium and add mackerel. Cover and cook, stirring occasionally (and carefully, so as to not break up the fish too much). Cook until sauce thickens, 20-30 minutes. Add eggs gently to dish and spoon sauce over. Serve hot.

*a civilized dinner (for Bill, who ate rice)*

*i brought out a small appetizer — delicious rolls that my aunt taught me of meat and potato chopped very fine and curried and wrapped in crepes and rolled in egg and bread crumb and fried till golden and*

*then some tandoori chicken baked in the oven which isn't quite the same as a tandoori oven, but you still get that gorgeous red like the brick that it would have been baked in so long ago plus a little*

*beef and potato curry, cooked for a long time so that the meat is very tender and the juices have mixed with the curry powder and the milk and the tomatoes to make a rich broth that flays your tongue and sends the endorphins shooting to your brain, so you somehow think that pain is pleasure and*

*rice of course, with*

*gulab jaman for dessert; cheese balls soaked in a honey-syrup so strong that more than two bites and you need almost as much water as you drank with the beef to wash away the sweetness...*

*oh dear.*

*you're a vegetarian?*

# Vegetables

Curried Beets
Carrots and Green Bean Curry
Cauliflower Curry
Mixed Vegetable Curry
Mild Potato Curry
Spicy Potato Curry
Lemon Masala Mushrooms
Chana Masala
Red Lentils with Spices

# Vegetables

If you talk to my college roommate Kirsten, she'll tell you that I used to claim that Sri Lankans never ate vegetables, and that this was just my excuse for not eating vegetables myself. Now, I don't think that's quite a fair recollection — I suspect what I was actually objecting to was salad, and that I was claiming that Sri Lankans didn't eat *raw* vegetables. Sadly, I can't remember for certain what I actually said in college. And I'm not sure it matters, since I'd be wrong either way.

Sri Lankans definitely do eat vegetables — growing up, I had vegetables with my rice every single night. Sometimes more than one kind of vegetable! And even if I avoided raw vegetables like poison, my mother was quite fond of salad, and made several dishes with raw vegetables (though the only recipes with raw veggies you'll find here are in the accompaniments section).

I still haven't learned to like salad much, and I admit that even living for years with vegetarian roommates, and then living in the Bay Area where every other person seemed to be a vegetarian, wasn't enough to teach me to love vegetables. I tend to not feel as if I've had a real dinner unless there's some meat or fish on the plate too. But I have (finally) learned to both enjoy, and cook, a few vegetables.

## Curried Beets
(30 min. — serves 4)

This dish has a lovely sweet flavor with just a hint of spice — beets have a higher sugar content than any other vegetable, and in the old days, when sugarcane wasn't available, sugar was often made from beets!

- 3 medium yellow onions, chopped fine
- 3 T vegetable oil
- 1/4 t. black mustard seed
- 1/4 t. cumin seed
- 4 large beets (about one lb.), peeled, cut in thick matchsticks
- 1 rounded t. salt
- 1 rounded t. turmeric
- 3 chopped green chilies
- 1 c. coconut milk, optional

1. Sauté onions in oil on high with mustard seed and cumin seeds until onions are golden/translucent (not brown). Add beets, salt, turmeric, and chilies.

2. Lower heat to medium and add enough water so the beets don't burn, approximately 1/2 c. to start (if you have the time, cook on low heat and don't add water at all — it'll taste better). Cover and cook, stirring frequently, until beets are cooked through, about 20 minutes.

3. Remove cover, add milk if desired, to provide a thicker gravy and added richness, and simmer, stirring, until well-blended. Serve hot.

## Carrots and Green Bean Curry
(30 min. — serves 4)

If you're at all familiar with nouvelle cuisine, you may find yourself a little distressed at the point in the recipe where it asks you to keep cooking. You'll watch all the lovely bright vegetable color disappear, to be replaced by far more muted tones. You'll be tempted to take the dish off the stove — but resist that temptation! Otherwise, your poor curry will be only half-cooked, and you'll be left with a sorry dish, caught 'twixt one thing and the other, and partaking of the worst of both.

- 3 medium yellow onions, chopped fine
- 3 T vegetable oil
- 1/4 t. black mustard seed
- 1/4 t. cumin seed
- 1/2 lb. green beans, cleaned and broken into bite-size pieces
- 3 large carrots, peeled and cut into bite-size pieces to match the beans
- 1 rounded t. salt
- 1 rounded t. turmeric
- 1/2 - 1 c. milk (can use soy milk or rice milk)

1. Sauté onions in oil on high with mustard seed and cumin seeds until onions are golden/translucent (not brown). Add carrots and green beans, turmeric, and salt. Cook on high, stirring frequently, until vegetables have lost their bright color and most of their moisture and begun to brown.

2. Add milk and turn heat down to low; simmer until blended, stirring constantly. Serve hot.

## Cauliflower Curry
(35 min. — serves 4)

The key to this dish is sautéing the cauliflower until it's fairly brown — the browned bits will be the tastiest. I generally like to serve this dish with beef curry; the slightly salty flavor complements the beef well.

  3 medium yellow onions, chopped fine
  3 T vegetable oil
  1/4 t. black mustard seed
  1/4 t. cumin seed
  1 medium cauliflower, chopped into bite-size pieces
  1 rounded t. salt
  1 rounded t. turmeric

1. Sauté onions in oil on high in a large frying pan with mustard seed and cumin seed until onions are golden/translucent (not brown). Add cauliflower, turmeric, and salt.

2. Cook on high, stirring frequently, until cauliflower is browned (mostly yellow, but with a fair bit of brown on the level parts). This takes a while — don't stop too early, or it won't be nearly as tasty. Serve hot.

## Mixed Vegetable Curry
(30 min. — serves 4)

This is essentially the same as the preceding cauliflower dish — it's more convenient, though, since you can keep the frozen veggies in your freezer and it thus doesn't require going to the grocery store, as long as you already have onions. And if you don't already have onions, well, you're going to have trouble cooking these dishes, is all I can say.

 3 medium yellow onions, chopped
 3 T vegetable oil
 1/4 t. black mustard seed
 1/4 t. cumin seed
 1 large package frozen mixed vegetables (bite-size pieces), thawed and drained
 1 rounded t. salt
 1 rounded t. turmeric

1. Sauté onions in oil on high with mustard seed and cumin seeds until onions are golden/translucent (not brown). Add mixed vegetables, turmeric, and salt.

2. Cook on medium-high, stirring periodically, until vegetables are cooked through and almost dry. Serve hot.

## Potatoes, Peas, and Tomatoes
(30 min. — serves 4)

This dish presents beautifully, with a mellow mix of golden potatoes, touches of muted red tomato, and a scattering of green peas. I love making this for dinner parties — but be sure you have a really large frying pan!

- 3 medium yellow onions, sliced
- 3 T vegetable oil
- 1/4 t. black mustard seed
- 1/4 t. cumin seed
- 3 small russet potatoes, peeled, sliced thickly
- 6 plum tomatoes, sliced thickly
- 1/2 lb. frozen peas, thawed and drained
- 1 rounded t. salt
- 1 rounded t. turmeric

1. Sauté onions in oil on high in a large frying pan with mustard seed and cumin seeds until onions are golden/translucent (not brown). Add potatoes, turmeric, and salt. Mix well.

2. Cook on medium-high, stirring occasionally, until potatoes are mostly cooked through and starting to stick. Add tomatoes and continue to stir.

3. When tomatoes are well-reduced, add peas and continue to stir. Cook until peas have lost their bright green color and much of their moisture; the ingredients should be well-blended in flavor, and the potatoes should be somewhat browned. Serve hot.

## Spicy Potato Curry
(30 min. — serves 4)

This is the vegetable dish I make most often (not actually a vegetable, I know), and I'm pretty sure it's Kevin's favorite. He eats it straight up in a bowl with a fork — but he's bolder than me.

   3 medium yellow onions, chopped
   3 T vegetable oil
   1/4 t. black mustard seed
   1/4 t. cumin seed
   1-2 T (or more to taste) red chili powder
   3 medium baking potatoes, peeled and cubed
   3 T ketchup
   1 rounded t. salt
   1/2 c. milk, optional

1. Sauté onions in oil on high with mustard seed and cumin seeds until onions are golden/translucent (not brown). Add chili powder and cook 1 minute, until you start to cough. Immediately add potatoes, ketchup, and salt.

2. Lower heat to medium and add enough water so the potatoes don't burn (enough to cover usually works well). Cover and cook, stirring periodically, until potatoes are cooked through, about 20 minutes.

3. Remove lid and simmer off any excess water; the resulting curry sauce should be fairly thick, so that the potatoes are coated with sauce, rather than swimming in liquid. Add milk, if desired, to thicken sauce and mellow spice level; stir until well-blended. Serve hot.

## Lemon-Masala Mushrooms
(20 min. — serves 4)

I have no idea where I learned this recipe; it's probably more Indian than Sri Lankan, given the garam masala, but I serve it all the time and it goes well with Sri Lankan curries, so here it is anyway. Don't cook the scallions too much at first or they'll lose all their color — they'll lose a lot anyway, both as the mushrooms cook, and once you add the lemon juice.

- 1 lb. button mushrooms, quartered
- 6 scallions (green onions), including greens, chopped fine
- 2-4 T butter (depending on how much you like butter; start with 2 and add more if desired)
- 1/2 rounded t. salt, or to taste
- 1/4 c. lemon juice, or to taste
- 1/2 rounded t. garam masala (Indian spice mix) (you can substitute Sri Lankan curry powder)

1. Sauté scallions in butter until slightly softened.

2. Add mushrooms and salt and cook on high heat until liquid is quite reduced, stirring frequently.

3. Add lemon juice and cook until juice is absorbed. Mushrooms should be glistening, but not sitting in liquid; they should be quite soft and slightly browned.

4. Remove from heat and stir in garam masala. Serve warm.

## Chana Masala
(35-45 min. — serves 4-6)

When I first met David, I taught him how to make Sri Lankan curries; he'd never cooked a curry before, but he took the dishes to heart and now makes curry often. I thought I'd borrow his yummy chana masala for you.

2 c. dried chickpeas
2 T vegetable oil
1 large yellow onion, sliced
4 garlic cloves, minced
ginger to match garlic, minced
4-6 plum tomatoes, chopped
3 small green chilies, chopped (optional)
6 oz. tomato paste
1/2 t. turmeric
1 t. salt, or to taste
2 t. chili powder, or to taste
3-4 t. garam masala
2 T lemon juice
1 bay leaf
chopped cilantro for garnish

1. Soak chickpeas overnight. Drain and cook until soft. Remove and mash 1 c. cooked chickpeas. Fry onions, garlic, and ginger in oil until onions are golden brown. Add tomato paste, tomatoes, mashed chickpeas, chilies, turmeric, salt, chili powder, 2 t. garam masala. Mix. Add 1/2 c. water; cook 5 min.

2. Add rest of chickpeas, bay leaf, water to cover. Cook 20 min., adding water if necessary. Add another 1-2 t. garam masala as desired. Add lemon juice. Garnish with cilantro. Serve hot.

## Red Lentils with Spices
(45 min. — serves 6-8)

Adapted by David from Julie Sahni's *Classic Indian Vegetarian and Grain Cooking*. David notes that this is a three-part recipe, but it's not as complicated as it might appear. First, start the lentils cooking; while that's working, fry up the onions, tomatoes and ginger in a separate pan, then add the onion-tomato ginger mix to the lentils once the lentils are ready. Then, using the same pan as used for the onions, briefly fry the spices in oil or ghee, and add that to the lentils at the end. This dish goes particularly well with coconut sambol.

*for the lentils:*
   1 1/2 c. red lentils
   6 small green chilies
   1/2 t. turmeric
   3 1/2 - 4 c. water
   1 1/2 t. salt, or to taste
*for the tomato-onion infusion:*
   2 T vegetable oil
   1 c. yellow onion, minced
   1 c. tomato, finely chopped
   1 T fresh ginger, grated or minced
*for the spice flavoring:*
   2 T vegetable oil
   1 T panch phoron
   4 bay leaves
   4 dry red chili pods (from Indian store)
   2 t. garlic, minced

1. Pick the lentils clean and wash in several changes of water. Put lentils, chilies, turmeric, salt and water in a 3.5 qt. cooking pot, mix well, and bring to a boil.

### Red Lentils with Spices (cont.)

2. Reduce heat to a medium simmer and cook, partially covered, for approximately 15-20 min., until most of the water has been absorbed; stir as needed to keep lentils from lumping together. Cover, reduce heat, and keep lentils at a low simmer, stirring occasionally.

3. While the lentils are in progress, heat oil in a large frying pan. Cook onions on medium-high, stirring often, until golden brown, 10-15 minutes. Add tomato and ginger and cook, stirring often, until tomatoes are cooked to a pulp, 5-10 minutes. Stir contents of pan into the lentils and scrape clean.

4. Heat 2 T oil in the frying pan to medium-high. When hot, add panch phoron and cook about 15 seconds, until cumin seeds start turning dark and/or mustard seed starts spattering. Add bay leaves and chili pods and cook another 20-30 seconds, stirring a bit, until chili pods turn dark. Turn off heat, add garlic, and cook another 20-30 seconds, until garlic starts to brown on the edges. Stir contents of pan into lentils and mix well. Serve hot.

# Accompaniments

Scallion Scrambled Eggs
Coconut Sambol
Seeni (Sugar) Sambol
Fried Eggplant Sambol
Cabbage Mallung
Leeks Fried with Chili
Rasam
Kiri Hodhi (Coconut Milk Gravy)
Cucumber-Tomato Raita
Mango-Ginger Chutney

# Accompaniments

It was years before I started making these; when I'm cooking just for myself, I generally can't be bothered (though occasionally I'll keep a batch of coconut sambol in the fridge and have a little with each curry meal). But these accompaniments have become quite a staple at my dinner parties. Many of them can be cooked very quickly — once you put the rice on, you still usually have time to make two of these. And they serve quite a few people — each person is meant to just take a little bit.

Of course, you can't guarantee that people will hold to that — my friends David and Heather tend to treat coconut sambol like a vegetable and just pile it on their plate. You can do that too, if you like — but just remember that coconut is definitely not diet food! It's full of rich, fatty goodness. A little extra cabbage mallung or chili-fried leeks, on the other hand, won't hurt your waistline at all.

Oh, and if you or your friends are chili wimps, some cucumber-tomato raita (or anything dairy-based, really) is an essential palate-cooler. Remember — water only spreads the fire.

## Scallion Scrambled Eggs
(10 min. — serves 8)

I know it looks like breakfast, but these eggs go great with rice or pittu. This dish is a particularly nice way to vary a vegetarian meal.

- 6 scallions (green onions), including greens, chopped fine
- 3 T vegetable oil
- 8 eggs, beaten
- 1 rounded t. dried dill weed
- 1 rounded t. salt
- 1 rounded t. black pepper

1. Mix eggs with dill, salt, and pepper.

2. Heat oil in a frying pan and sauté scallions on medium-high until golden.

3. Pour egg mixture into pan and cook gently until dry. Flip (in pieces, if necessary) and cook other side until lightly browned.

### Coconut Sambol
(10 min. — serves 8)

This is the accompaniment I make most often – it goes with almost anything. You can adjust the chili powder/paprika ratio for more or less spice, as you desire.

- 1 c. desiccated unsweetened coconut
- 1 flat t. salt
- 1 rounded t. red chili powder
- 2 rounded t. paprika
- 2-3 T lemon juice, to taste
- 1 medium onion, minced
- 3 T hot milk

1. Combine coconut, salt, chili powder, and paprika in a bowl.

2. Sprinkle with lemon juice, onion, and milk.

3. Mix well with your hands, squeezing ingredients together so that the coconut is evenly moistened.

4. Pile into small bowl and serve.

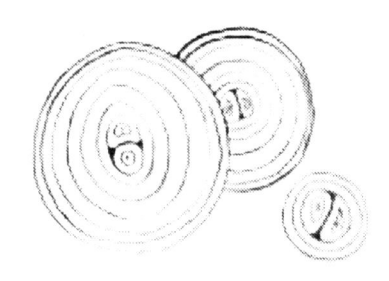

## Seeni (Sugar) Sambol
(1 hr. — serves 8)

A lot of work, but oh, so tasty!

> 1/2 c. oil
> 4 medium yellow onions, sliced fine
> 2 rounded t. red chili powder
> 2 T white vinegar
> salt to taste
> 2 rounded t. sugar

1. Heat oil in a large frying pan and sauté onions very slowly, stirring occasionally until soft and transparent, with a gold tinge. It's important to cook the onions slowly — all the liquid in the onion must evaporate if you want the sambol to keep well. Made properly, this dish can keep for several weeks, so you can enjoy a little with each meal for quite a long time.

2. When the onions are ready, add chili powder and vinegar. Stir thoroughly, cover, and simmer for 10 minutes.

3. Uncover pan and continue simmering, stirring occasionally, until liquid evaporates and oil starts to separate from other ingredients. Season to taste with salt.

4. Remove from heat, stir in sugar, and allow to cool before putting in a jar. Use in small quantities.

## Fried Eggplant Sambol
(1 hr. prep, 20 min. cooking — serves 8)

I started making these for the *Strange Horizons* writing workshops, when I realized that I had vegans to feed and not enough vegan dishes to feed them. They're quite popular with non-vegans too!

 1 medium purple eggplant
 1 rounded t. salt
 1 rounded t. turmeric
 oil for deep frying
 3 fresh green chilies, seeded and chopped fine
 1 medium yellow onion, sliced thin
 lemon juice to taste

1. Slice eggplant thinly, rub with salt and turmeric, spread on a few layers of paper towels and let sit at least 1 hr. Bitter water will rise to the surface of the eggplant; blot that water with more paper towels. This will make for much tastier eggplant.

2. Heat about an inch of oil in a deep frying pan and fry eggplant slices slowly until brown on both sides and slightly crisp. Lift out with Chinese spider (or any slotted or mesh spoon) and put in a dry bowl.

3. Mix with remaining ingredients; serve warm.

## Cabbage Mallung

(15 min. — serves 8)

Sri Lankans don't eat salads, as such, but this dish is perhaps as close as we come. A mallung can be made with any shredded green leaves.

   8 oz. cabbage
   1 medium yellow onion, minced
   2 fresh green chilies, seeded and chopped
   1/4 rounded t. turmeric
   1/4 rounded t. fresh ground black pepper
   1 rounded t. salt
   1/2 c. desiccated unsweetened coconut

1. Shred cabbage finely. Wash well, drain, and put into a large saucepan. Don't worry about drying the water clinging to the cabbage — you actually want that water to help steam the cabbage.

2. Add all the other ingredients except the coconut. Cover and cook gently until cabbage is tender, stirring periodically.

3. Uncover, add coconut, stir well, and when the liquid in the pan has been absorbed by the coconut, remove from heat. Allow to cool before serving.

## Leeks Fried with Chili
(50 min. — serves 8)

I think Kevin still doesn't quite believe that we're supposed to use the green parts of the leek in this dish – in most European leek dishes, you just use the white part. But you really do use the greens here, I promise.

4 medium leeks
1/4 c. oil
1/2 rounded t. turmeric
1 1/2 rounded t. red chili powder
1 rounded t. salt

1. Rinse dirt off outside of leeks. Discard any tough or withered leaves, but use the green portions as well as the white. With a sharp knife, slice leeks thinly.

2. Wash the sliced leeks very thoroughly. The soil trapped between the leaves won't actually taste particularly bad, but the grittiness is unpleasant. I recommend not simply rinsing the sliced leeks while they're sitting in a colander — rather, put them in a large bowl of water and wash them vigorously, changing the water at least three times. This is labor-intensive, but well worth it.

3. Heat oil in a large saucepan and add the leeks. Sauté, stirring for 5 minutes, then add the remaining ingredients and stir until well-blended.

4. Cover and cook over low heat for 30 min., stirring occasionally. The leeks will reduce in volume. Uncover and cook, stirring, until liquid evaporates and leeks appear slightly oily. Serve hot.

## Rasam
(20 min. — serves 8)

I don't make this often myself, but it's one of my mother's favorite dishes. For a very simple meal, serve it to sip with plain rice, with perhaps a little sambol.

- 1 T tamarind paste
- 1 c. hot water
- 2 cloves garlic, sliced
- 3/4 rounded t. fresh ground black pepper
- 1 rounded t. ground cumin
- 4 c. cold water
- 2 rounded t. salt
- 2 T chopped fresh coriander leaves
- 2 t. vegetable oil
- 1 rounded t. black mustard seeds
- 8 curry leaves

1. Dissolve tamarind paste in hot water.

2. Put tamarind liquid, garlic, pepper, cumin, water, salt, and coriander into a saucepan and bring to a boil.

3. Lower heat and simmer for 10 minutes.

4. In another pan, heat the oil and sauté the mustard seeds and curry leaves until leaves are toasted. Add to the simmering liquid and serve hot.

## Kiri Hodhi (Coconut Milk Gravy)
(30 min. — serves 8)

This is a delicious traditional accompaniment for stringhoppers (page 92), served with a little coconut sambol. When I last visited Sri Lanka, that was one of my favorite meals to have for breakfast, in the very early morning at the hotel, when I was still jet-lagged. It's quite soothing.

1 T fenugreek seeds
1 large yellow onion, sliced
12 curry leaves
1 small stick cinnamon
2 fresh green chilies, seeded and chopped
1/4 rounded t. turmeric
1/2 rounded t. salt
2 c. coconut milk + 2 c. water
2 russet potatoes, peeled and cut in big chunks
2 c. undiluted coconut milk
3 hard-boiled eggs, cut in half lengthwise
lemon juice to taste

1. Put all the ingredients except the undiluted milk, eggs, and lemon juice in a saucepan. Simmer on very low heat until onions are reduced to a pulp and the milk has thickened.

2. Stir well, add thick coconut milk, and heat without bringing dish to a boil. Stir in lemon juice, salt to taste, and then carefully add the eggs. Simmer a minute or two longer, stirring, and then serve hot.

## Cucumber-Tomato Raita
(10 min. — serves 8)

I'm afraid I've never picked up the habit of eating yogurt with curry (I prefer my yogurt with fruit and honey), but many of my friends swear by raita, and the ones who have trouble with the spiciness of some of the dishes really appreciate the cooling properties of yogurt. I usually make some raita to accompany a spicy meal when serving guests.

- 1 medium cucumber
- 2-4 plum tomatoes, coarsely chopped
- 2 fresh green chilies, seeded and chopped (optional)
- 1/2 t. salt
- fresh ground black pepper to taste
- 1 1/2 c. yogurt (full-fat ideally)

1. Grate cucumber coarsely; squeeze out excess water.

2. Mix all ingredients well; serve cold.

## Mango-Ginger Chutney
(25 min. — serves 8)

You don't actually need to cook a chutney — you can just chop up some fruit and mix it with spices and serve; that's quite common in Sri Lanka. But I prefer a more blended chutney, with a mellower flavor.

- 3 fresh mangoes, peeled and chopped
- 1 rounded t. salt
- 1 c. malt vinegar
- 3 dried red chilies (optional)
- 3 T fresh ginger, peeled and chopped fine
- 3/4 - 1 c. sugar
- 1/3 c. sultanas (golden raisins)
- 1 rounded t. garam masala

1. Put mango pieces in a large bowl and sprinkle with salt.

2. Remove stalks and seeds from chilies (if used) and soak chilies in a little vinegar for 10 minutes. Combine vinegar, ginger, and chilies in a blender and blend (you can alternatively pound the chilies with a mortar and pestle and grate the ginger in).

3. Put blended mixture in a stainless steel pan with garam masala and sugar and bring to a boil. Simmer, uncovered, for 15 minutes.

4. Add mangoes and sultanas and simmer until thick and syrupy. Cool and serve.

*Note: You can substitute green apples, pears, apricots, etc. for mangoes. Or mix and match!*

*Mambalam, nala mambalam,*
*Mama thantha mambalam,*
*Munjel vannai mambalam,*
*Munum veesum mambalam.*

Mango, nice mango,
Uncle gave me a mango,
It is a yellow mango,
A sweet-smelling mango.

— *Tamil children's rhyme*

# Rice and Breads

Golden Rice Pilaf
Vegetable or Chicken Biryani
Pittu
Uppuma
Kottu Roti
Hoppers
Stringhoppers

## Golden Rice Pilaf
(20 min. — serves 4-6)

Here's where I cheat. When I'm having a party, I'd often like to serve biryani, as my mother would — but making biryani properly is a fair bit of work, and sometimes I just don't have time. So I often make this instead. To be traditional, you'd use basmati rice, which is quite fragrant — but I admit, I prefer short-grain Japanese rice, and almost always cook with it instead. It works quite well — and my sisters like it too. Brown rice will also work.

- 2 c. uncooked rice
- 4 c. water
- 1/4 - 1/2 c. sultanas (golden raisins)
- 1/4 - 1/2 c. cashews
- 1 T butter
- 1/4 t. salt
- 1-2 drops rose essence
- 1/2 t. saffron (you can cheat with 1/4 t. turmeric for a similar color, but it won't taste right)

1. Combine all ingredients in a large pot and bring to a boil.

2. Cover and turn heat down to simmer until rice is cooked and the water is absorbed, approximately 15 minutes.

*Note: If you're willing to go to slightly more trouble, toast the cashews separately in a dry pan (be careful not to burn them) and stir them in at the end, when the rice is almost cooked. They'll be crisper and nuttier.*

## Vegetable or Chicken Biryani
(2 hrs — serves 6-8)

If you can take the time, this dish is delicious to eat all on its own; it's also perfect for a fancy dinner party. For the vegetarian version, skip the chicken curry and stir in a cup of vegetable broth before baking. It also doubles well in a large casserole dish.

- 1 recipe chicken curry (page 42)
- 1 recipe golden rice pilaf (page 85)
- 3 medium russet potatoes, peeled and cubed
- 3 medium yellow onions, sliced
- 1 t. salt
- 3 T vegetable oil

1. Sauté onions in oil on high heat, stirring frequently, until golden.

2. Add potatoes and salt and sauté, adding more oil if necessary, until potatoes are golden and slightly browned. Remove from heat.

3. Combine potatoes, chicken curry, and rice in a large casserole dish. Cover and bake at 350 degrees for approximately 45 min., until flavors are well-blended. Serve hot.

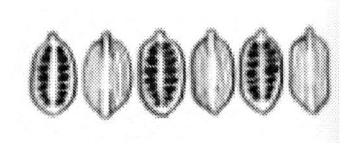

**Pittu**
(20 min. — serves 4-6)

Pittu is one of many dishes we eat instead of rice; it's tastiest when made with two cups of fresh coconut, but works just fine with reconstituted desiccated coconut. We would make this in a bamboo cylinder steamer; you can improvise a cylindrical steamer by using a tall narrow can (about the size of a coffee can) and punching holes in the bottom. But it also works fine in a regular steamer; it just won't have the characteristic cylindrical shape when served. If you're using a regular metal steamer, wrap the crumbly dough loosely in a few layers of thick paper towel or a clean dish towel before steaming, to keep it from getting water-logged.

2 c. desiccated coconut
3/4 - 1 c. hot water (I use about 7/8 c.)
2 c. all-purpose flour (or 1 c. flour + 1 c. fine
  semolina, for a more traditional recipe)
3/4 t. salt

1. In a large bowl, combine the desiccated coconut and water; work gently with your fingers until all the coconut is well-moistened (if you're using fresh grated coconut, you shouldn't need any water).

2. Add flour and salt to coconut in bowl, and rub it gently with the fingertips until it forms fine crumbs (as you would for the topping of an apple crisp).

3. Fill steamer with mixture and press it down lightly. Steam in a large pot over boiling water for 10-15 minutes, until dough is thoroughly cooked. Turn onto plate and serve hot.

## Uppuma
(20 min. — serves 4-6)

If you're in a terrible hurry, skip the whole onion-frying thing — the great thing about uppuma is that you can make it in five minutes, as opposed to the twenty you'd need for rice. On the other hand, it's much tastier if you take the time to do it properly. Don't be thrown by the Cream o' Wheat — that's just a brand name for farina, a type of wheat. If I had just listed farina, would you have known where to look for it?

- 2 small yellow onions, chopped fine
- 3 green chilies, seeded and chopped
- 1 T fenugreek (methi seeds)
- 2-8 tablespoons butter
- 3 c. water
- 1 rounded t. salt
- 2 c. farina (Cream o' Wheat)

1. Sauté onions in butter until onions are golden. Add chilies and cook a minute longer. Add fenugreek and cook 1 additional minute.

2. Add water and salt; bring to a boil.

3. Turn down to a simmer and quickly pour in the farina, stirring constantly, making sure all the farina is moistened. Remove from heat and allow dish to sit for a few minutes before serving. Serve warm — delicious with fish.

*Note: The measurement on the butter is so imprecise because while you can get by with only two tablespoons (or with oil instead), it'll be tastier if you use more.*

## Kottu Roti
(90 min. — serves 4-6)

This dish is crazy addictive. It's basically an entire meal in one dish; a little meat, a little bread, a little vegetable. Just like Thanksgiving stuffing!

    1 lb. curried chicken, beef, mutton, pork or a combination of meats, cut into bite-size cubes
    5 large flour tortillas, cut in finger-size strips
    1 whole head of garlic, peeled and chopped
    2 T fresh ginger, chopped fine
    2-4 green chilies, seeded and chopped fine
    1 large leek, cleaned well and chopped fine
    4 oz. carrots, grated
    1 medium yellow onion, finely chopped
    2-3 eggs, beaten
    6 fresh curry leaves (optional)
    1 heaping t. salt
    1/4 T ground black pepper
    3 T vegetable oil
    lemon wedges for garnish

1. Fry onions, garlic, ginger, curry leaves, and green chilies in oil. When the onions are transparent, add salt, black pepper, leeks, and carrots.

2. When the vegetables are almost cooked through, add the tortillas. Stir until well-blended. (If it starts sticking too much, add a little extra oil or butter.)

3. Add the beaten eggs and fry, stirring, until the eggs are cooked, a minute or two. Stir in the meat curry until well-blended, a few minutes. Serve hot with fresh lemon wedges. Squeeze juice over.

## Hoppers
(90 min. — serves 6)

When I think of classic Sri Lankan food, this is the dish that comes to mind – bowl-shaped pancakes, made in a special dish somewhat like a small wok, but with a more hemispherical shape. The sides of the pancake are crisp and thin, the bottom is rich and doughy. You can buy the pan in some Indian stores, but unless you'll be making them often, I'd just use a wok.

- 1 oz. dried yeast
- 2 c. warm water
- 1 1/2 t. sugar
- 3 c. flour (I use half rice flour, half all-purpose flour, but entirely rice flour is more traditional)
- 2 t. salt
- 2 c. coconut milk

1. Sprinkle yeast over warm water, stir to dissolve, add the sugar, and leave for approximately 10 min. The yeast should froth slightly; if it doesn't, start over with a new package of yeast.

2. Put both flours and salt in a large bowl. Add coconut milk to the yeast and stir the mixture into the dry ingredients to form a smooth, thick batter. Allow to stand overnight, or put in a warm (turned off) oven for one hour until mixture rises and doubles in bulk.

3. Stir; add some warm water or milk if necessary for an easy pouring consistency. The batter should pour well, but also be thick enough to cover the sides of the pan with a very thin coating when the batter is swirled in the pan, to crepe consistency.

## Hoppers (cont.)

4. Heat the pan/wok over low heat, oil lightly, and pour in about 1/3 c. of batter. Pick up the pan and swirl it around so that the batter coats the pan about 2/3 of the way up the sides. The rest of the batter should settle into the bottom; add more batter to the center if you prefer a thicker spongy layer. Cover pan and cook on low heat for about 5 min. The upper edges should turn a pale toasted brown; uncover and cook a little longer if necessary. Slip from pan onto a wire rack; keep warm in oven while you continue to make more. Serve hot with a rich meat or fish curry.

*Breakfast variation:* Before covering the pan, crack an egg into the center and replace lid. Egg will steam-cook. Serve with coconut sambol (page 73) or seeni sambol (page 74).

*Dessert variation:* Mix 1 c. coconut milk with 2 T sugar or honey; simmer in a small pan until somewhat thickened. After your hopper has cooked for two minutes, pour in a few T of sweetened coconut milk (mix a little honey or sugar into the milk). Delicious!

## Stringhoppers
(30 min. — serves 4)

Okay, this one's an experiment for the bold. Stringhoppers are nummy, but are generally made with a bunch of special equipment. Here's a modified version that you can make with bamboo mats, a steamer, and a vermicelli press. Or you can go to the Indian store and try to find a stringhopper press and the rest of the steaming equipment.

- 3 c. rice flour
- 1 1/2 t. salt
- 1 c. less 2 T boiling water (or as needed)

1. Mix salt and flour in a bowl, then slowly add the hot water and work into a soft dough. Place the dough in a vermicelli press, and press the plunger to squeeze small, flat noodle patties onto small bamboo mats. (Whatever mats you use need to be open enough to allow for steam to pass through evenly.)

2. Place the mats in a steamer. Steam until strings are fully cooked and springy in texture, about 10 min.

3. Remove stringhoppers from the steamer and serve hot with coconut sambol (page 73) and kiri hodhi (page 79) for a light breakfast. Alternatively, serve with spicy curry for dinner.

*Come to me.*
*I will make you rice.*

*Thick, white, sticky rice,*
*clinging to your fingertips.*
*Dark, wild rice,*
*scented like fields in autumn.*

*Slender grains of basmati rice,*
*aromatic, rich with rose essence,*
*saffron-gold-threaded,*
*graced by sultanas,*
*almonds and cashews...*

*Come to me, and I will feed you rice*
*made by my own small hands.*

# Drinks

Mango Lassi
Falooda
Chai Tea

## Mango Lassi
(10 min. — serves 4)

Some people like their mango lassi very sweet; some like it hardly sweet at all. That decision is best left up to the individual cook.

   several ice cubes
   1 c. plain yogurt (more if desired)
   1 jar (or 1 can) fresh mango pieces (roughly 48 oz.)
   a few drops rose essence
     (careful not to add too much!)
   3-5 c. iced water
   1/4 c. or more (or less) honey

1. Crush ice in blender.

2. Add yogurt, mango, rose essence, and blend.

3. Add 3 c. water and blend — stop blender and taste, add more water if desired until preferred consistency is reached.

4. Add honey to taste and blend.

## Falooda
(20 min. — serves 4)

Okay, I admit, the tulsi seeds kind of weird me out. But this is one of my mother's favorite drinks – cooling and festive.

agar-agar jelly, diced (see below)
3 c. sugar
2 c. water
20 drops rose essence
ice cold milk as required, about 1 c. for each serving
crushed ice
soaked tulsi seeds (optional)

Jelly:
3 c. water
4 rounded t. agar-agar powder or 1 c. soaked agar-agar strands
6 T sugar
12 drops rose essence
1 rounded t. liquid red food coloring
1 rounded t. liquid green food coloring

1. Make syrup: Put sugar and water in a saucepan and cook over gentle heat until sugar dissolves. Cool. Add rose flavoring and red coloring. You have now made rose syrup.

2. Make jelly: Measure water into a saucepan and sprinkle agar-agar powder over. If agar-agar strands are used, soak at least 2 hours in cold water, then drain and measure 1 c. loosely packed. Bring to a boil and simmer gently, stirring, until agar-agar dissolves. Powder takes about 10 minutes and the strands take longer, about 25-30 minutes.

**Falooda (cont.)**

3. Add sugar and dissolve, remove from heat, cool slightly, and add rose flavoring. Divide mixture between two large shallow dishes and color one red and the other green. Leave to set. When quite cold and firm, cut with a sharp knife first into fine strips, then across into small dice.

4. Put about 2 T each of diced jelly and rose syrup into a tall glass, fill up with ice-cold milk and crushed ice. Float some soaked tulsi seeds on top if desired.

## Chai Tea
(15 min. — serves 4)

I've been delighted to see bookstore coffee shops across America start serving chai; as someone who rarely drinks coffee, it's lovely having other options. But I admit to often being disappointed in their tea — it's often made from powder, and is painfully grainy. And even when it's smooth, it's generally under-spiced and over-sweetened. This is chai the way I like to make it when I'm feeling indulgent. Though I admit, most of the time at home, I just use Stash's ready-made Chai Tea bags, which make surprisingly tasty tea.

- 4 c. milk
- 6 black tea bags (I recommend Twinings Ceylon Breakfast)
- 2 sticks cinnamon
- 5 cloves
- 5 cardamom pods
- 5 slices fresh ginger, sliced cross-wise
- sugar or honey to taste, about 2-4 t.

1. In a saucepan, bring milk almost to a boil (but not quite).

2. Turn down heat and add tea, cinnamon, cloves, cardamom, and ginger. Heat tea and spices in milk until well-brewed (5-10 min). The mixture should be aromatic and have a light-brown color.

3. Add sugar or honey to taste; stir until well-blended.

4. Strain mixture through a fine sieve into four mugs. Serve hot.

## Sweets

Milk Toffee

Vattalappam (Spiced Coconut Custard)

Lemon-Chai Rice Pudding

Rich Cake (Wedding/Christmas Cake)

## Milk Toffee
(30 min. — serves dozens)

This is a classic dessert, but this particular recipe is from one of my aunts, who swore that it was an ancient family secret; I swore in return that I would keep the secret, and so I have now broken my sworn word to bring you this dessert. Be grateful — and be careful! The sugar syrup gets *extremely* hot.

  2 cans condensed milk
  1/2 lb. - 3/4 lb. cashews
  1 1/2 lb. sugar
  1/2 can (condensed milk can) water
  2 T vanilla
  1 stick butter (preferably salted)

1. Grease a 9" x 12" cake pan. Put sugar, water, and condensed milk together on high in large nonstick pot.

2. When the mixture starts boiling, lower heat to medium. Cook for 5-10 minutes (no need to stir). When it starts to thicken (but is still watery), add cashews and stir. When it thickens a bit more, add vanilla and stir.

3. When it starts sticking to the pan, add 1 stick of butter and mix it in. As soon as the butter melts, take pot off stove and immediately pour into buttered pan, using a wooden spoon to guide toffee.

4. Crumple up a ball of saran wrap; use it to protect your hand and pound toffee flat. 5-10 minutes later, try cutting it. If it doesn't stick to your knife, you can cut it into small pieces.

## Vattalappam (Spiced Coconut Custard)
(90 min. — serves 4-6)

Similar to flan (or crème brulee), but lighter and more spiced. Do be sure to chill them; the flavors come out more when you do.

- 4 eggs
- 1/2 c. firmly packed dark brown sugar
- 1/2 c. maple syrup
- 0 – 1/2 c. water (depending on whether you'd prefer it firmly set or soft with sweet liquid)
- 1 1/2 c. coconut milk
- 3/4 c. evaporated milk
- 1/2 t. ground cardamom
- 1/4 t. ground mace
- pinch ground cloves
- 1 T rose water

1. Preheat oven to 325 degrees.

2. Beat eggs slightly (not frothy). Dissolve sugar in water over a low heat and then cool slightly (enough so that the hot syrup doesn't accidentally cook the eggs). Add sugar syrup and maple syrup to beaten eggs, add the coconut milk, and stir to blend well.

3. Strain through a fine strainer into a large bowl with spout (a 4 c. measuring cup works well). Add evaporated milk, spices, and rose water, stirring well to blend. Pour into individual 4 oz. custard cups. Put custard cups in a baking dish; put dish in the oven and add water to come halfway up sides of cups; bake until set, approximately 1 1/4 hours.

4. Chill thoroughly before serving.

## Lemon-Chai Rice Pudding
(45 min. — serves 4-6)

I invented this dish while visiting Roshani in Milwaukee; she was moving up there for a new job, and had very little in her cupboards. She did have chai tea bags, fresh lemons, rice, honey, and milk — plenty to make a delectable dessert! Here's a slightly fancier version.

    4 c. milk
    6 black tea bags (I recommend Twinings Ceylon Breakfast)
    2 sticks cinnamon
    5 cloves
    5 cardamom pods
    5 slices fresh ginger
    sugar or honey to taste, about 2-4 t.
    1 1/2 c. rice
    juice of one fresh lemon

1. In a saucepan, bring milk almost to a boil (but not quite). Turn down heat and add tea, cinnamon, cloves, cardamom, and ginger. Simmer tea and spices in milk until well-brewed. The mixture should be aromatic and have a light-brown color.

3. Add sugar or honey to taste; stir until well-blended.

4. Strain mixture through a fine sieve into a saucepan. Add rice, bring almost to a boil, and then turn down to a simmer. Cook, stirring frequently, until rice is cooked through and milk is well-reduced. Stir in lemon juice (and more sugar/honey if desired) and serve hot.

## Rich Cake (Wedding/Christmas Cake)
(3 hr. — serves dozens)

There's a cultural myth that fruitcake is some horrid dry thing that gets pressed upon you by similarly dried-up old aunts. But a real fruitcake, the kind that's descended from a traditional British steamed figgy pudding, is dense, rich, moist, fruity, pleasantly alcoholic, and the kind of cake you sneak into the kitchen after midnight to steal extra bites of. Trust me.

- 8 oz. seedless raisins
- 12 oz. sultanas (golden raisins)
- 16 oz. mixed dried fruit (cherries, cranberries, figs, mango, apricot, peach, pear — *not pineapple*), larger pieces chopped to roughly raisin-size
- 8 oz. candied ginger
- 8 oz. ginger preserves
- 8 oz. apricot or fig preserves
- 2 oz. mixed peel
- 8 oz. raw cashews (or blanched almonds)
- 1/4 c. brandy
- 12 oz. butter
- 12 oz. superfine sugar
- 12 egg yolks
- 2 t. grated lemon zest
- 1/2 t. ground cardamom
- 1 t. ground cinnamon
- 1 t. grated nutmeg
- 3/4 t. ground cloves
- 2 T vanilla essence
- 1 T almond essence
- 2 t. rose essence
- 1/2 c. honey
- 8 oz. fine semolina
- 6 egg whites

## Rich Cake (cont.)

1. Line a 10" square cake tin with three alternating layers each of newspaper and brown paper, then two layers of wax paper. Brush liberally with melted butter.

2. Chop dried fruit. Drain syrup from preserves and chop. Chop mixed peel. Chop nuts finely (food processor recommended). Combine fruits and nuts in your second-largest bowl, sprinkle with brandy, cover and leave while mixing cake. This can be done the day before, allowing the fruit more time to soak in the brandy.

3. In the biggest bowl you have, cream butter and sugar until light. Add egg yolks one at a time, beating well. Add grated zest, spices, flavorings, and honey and mix well. Add semolina and beat until well combined, then mix in fruit with both hands.

4. Whip egg whites until stiff and fold through mixture. Turn into prepared cake tin and bake in preheated 275 degree oven for 2 1/4 hours — cover the cake with paper after the first hour to prevent over-browning.

5. Cool completely, preferably overnight, then remove paper and wrap cake in foil; if you like, you can sprinkle a few more tablespoons of brandy over the cold cake before wrapping it.

## Rich Cake (cont.)

6. Alternatively, frost the top of the cake with almond paste and then cut the cake into small rectangles (about two fingers wide) and wrap each individually in wax paper and colored foil — this is the presentation we would use for weddings, where little girls would carry baskets of the cake around at the end of the wedding and give a little cake to each guest to take home.

*Note: This cake can be kept in an airtight tin for a year or longer. It just gets richer and moister — I recommend making it no later than October if you want to serve it at Christmas.*

## About the Author

Mary Anne Mohanraj (www.mamohanraj.com) is the author of *Silence and the Word*, *Kathryn in the City*, *The Classics Professor*, and *Torn Shapes of Desire*. She served as editor for *The Best of Strange Horizons: Year One*, *Aqua Erotica*, *Wet*, and *Blowing Kisses*. Mary Anne has been published in a multitude of anthologies and magazines, including *Best American Erotica 1999*, and *Best Women's Erotica 2000* and *2001*. She serves as editor-in-chief for the Hugo-nominated speculative fiction webzine *Strange Horizons* and as director of *The Speculative Literature Foundation*. Mary Anne is a doctoral student in Fiction and Literature at the University of Utah, and currently lives in Greektown, Chicago.

## About the Illustrator

Rachel Hartman (www.amyunbounded.com) is the author, illustrator, and publisher of the award-winning *Amy Unbounded* comic book series. Her first trade paperback collection, *Amy Unbounded: Belondweg Blossoming*, came out in 2002. Rachel's comic strips and articles have also appeared in *Dark Tower*, *Spark Generators II*, and on the *Strange Horizons* and *Sequential Tart* webzines. Her current projects include writing a young adult fantasy novel and raising a rambunctious baby boy. Rachel Hartman lives in Vancouver.